तेजोमय ग्रन्थ माला

हनुमान चालीसा
Hanumāna Cālīsā

* * *

Commentary by
Swami Tejomayananda

Central Chinmaya Mission Trust

•

Originally printed in USA

Reprint in India from Nov 2008 to March 2010 - 21000 copies

Revised Edition - Nov 2011 - 3000 copies

Reprint - January 2013 - 3000 copies

•

Published by:

Central Chinmaya Mission Trust

Sandeepany Sadhanalaya

Saki Vihar Road, Mumbai 400072, India

Tel.: +91-22-2857 2367, 2857 5806

Fax: +91-22-2857 3065

Email: ccmtpublications@chinmayamission.com

Website: www.chinmayamission.com

•

Distribution Centre in USA:

Chinmaya Mission West

Publications Division

560 Bridgetown Pike, Langhorne, PA 19053, USA

Tel.: (215) 396-0390 Fax: (215) 396-9710

Email: publications@chinmayamission.org

Website: www.chinmayapublications.org

•

Printed by:

Repro India Ltd.

•

Price: ₹ 70/-

•

ISBN 978-81-7597-026-7

CTP

PUBLISHER'S NOTE

Śrī Hanumāna is the favourite of all Hindus, especially children for whom he is a superhero. *Hanumānacālīsā* is one of the most popular texts and is chanted by millions all over India. Śrī Hanumāna's stories and superhuman deeds are inspiring people even outside the Hindu fold. A recent animation movie on him became an instant hit.

Pūjya Gurudev Swami Chinmayananda installed the 23 feet tall Śrī Hanumāna idol at Siddhabāri (cover page) even before the Śrī Rāma temple was built saying, 'Śrī Hanumāna will bring His Lord!' This year is the Silver Jubilee of the installation of that most beautiful idol (see cover page). Every five years, there is a mastakābhiṣeka performed for Śrī Hanumāna in which thousands participate. In October this year, there will be the mahāmastakābhiṣeka commemorating the 25th year of installation.

On this occasion we take pleasure in bringing out the 'new look' version of Pūjya Guruji's commentary on the *Hanumānacālīsā*.

Pūjya Guruji's beautiful composition in praise of Śrī Hanumāna at Siddhabāri (Hanumāna Stuti) gives an apt finishing touch to this book.

The beatutiful cover page is designed by Shri Sunil Sachdeva, Delhi. Smt. Tripta Bhalla painstakingly typed out the manuscript. We thank them for their Guru sevā and pray for His grace on them.

May we all imbibe the great virtues of devotion and service from Śrī Hanumāna.

Mumbai **CENTRAL CHINMAYA MISSION TRUST**

Transliteration and Pronunciation Guide

In the book, Devanāgarī characters are transliterated according to the scheme adopted by the International Congress of Orientalists at Athens in 1912. In it one fixed pronunciation value is given to each letter; f, q, w, x and z are not called to use. An audio recording of this guide is available at http://chinmayamission.com/scriptures.php. According to this scheme:

Devanāgarī	Translit-eration	Sounds Like	Devanāgarī	Translit-eration	Sounds Like
अ	a	son	ढ्	ḍh	adhesive*
आ	ā	father	ण्	ṇ	under*
इ	i	different	त्	t	tabla
ई	ī	feel	थ्	th	thumb
उ	u	full	द्	d	this
ऊ	ū	boot	ध्	dh	Gandhi
ऋ	ṛ	rhythm*	न्	n	nose
ॠ	ṝ	**	प्	p	pen
ऌ	ḷ	**	फ्	ph	phantom*
ए	e	evade	ब्	b	boil
ऐ	ai	delight	भ्	bh	abhor
ओ	o	core	म्	m	mind
औ	au	now	य्	y	yes
क्	k	calm	र्	r	right
ख्	kh	khan	ल्	l	love
ग्	g	gate	व्	v	very
घ्	gh	ghost	श्	ś	shut
ङ्	ṅ	ankle*	ष	ṣ	sugar
च्	c	chuckle	स्	s	simple
छ्	ch	witch*	ह्	h	happy
ज्	j	justice	ं	ṁ	improvise
झ्	jh	Jhansi	ः	ḥ	**
ञ्	ñ	banyan	क्ष्	kṣ	action
ट्	ṭ	tank	त्र्	tr	three*
ठ्	ṭh	**	ज्ञ्	jñ	gnosis
ड्	ḍ	dog	ऽ	'	a silent 'a'

* These letters don't have an exact English equivalent. An approximation is given here.
** These sounds cannot be approximated in English words.

INTRODUCTION

In this world, it is almost impossible for any individual to lead a life that is above criticism – just or unjust. If we study the great epic, *Rāmāyaṇa*, we find that even Lord Rāma and Mother Sītā did not escape criticism from their own subjects, even though unjust. The only person in *Rāmāyaṇa* who succeeded in accomplishing this is Śrī Hanumāna – one of the greatest devotees of the Lord. We do not find a single incident wherein Śrī Hanumāna has committed any mistake and got blamed for any act of his. He is the very embodiment of wisdom, devotion and service. This noble son of Vāyū (Wind-god) has innumerable virtues.

It is easy to recognize the importance and the service of the sun throughout the day. It is more valued because it is not available in the night. But the wind remains with us 24 hours of the day, serving all beings without any desire for recognition and appreciation for its service. We, therefore, do not pay much respect or give much attention to it and take its existence for granted. Śrī Hanumāna has imbibed from his father, the Wind-god, this rare and noble virtue of serving all without a trace of pride in his heart. He crossed the ocean, entered the formidable Laṅkā and burnt it, found Mother Sītā and killed the demons who served Rāvaṇa. He served Lord Rāma in numerous such ways. The Lord Himself felt overwhelmed by his service and was filled with extreme love and gratitude for Śrī Hanumāna. He expressed His feelings and praised Śrī Hanumāna. But on hearing his own praise, Śrī Hanumāna, like a true devotee of the Lord, fell at His feet with tears in his eyes and gave all credit for his achievements to the Lord alone. What a noble and inspiring ideal of service coupled with utmost humility!

We are advised to imbibe from Śrī Hanumāna, this rare quality of serving one's master with unswerving faith and devotion. But little do we realize that before doing so, it is of utmost importance to know who should really be our master. One who is the Lord of the universe and in serving whom one's potential divinity comes to shine forth, He alone can be one's true master. This is revealed in the life of Śrī Hanumāna. Before meeting Lord Rāma he was serving Sugrīva and his powers remained dormant at that time. Sugrīva was not able to manifest them. Lord Rāma did so by His sheer grace. We see that Sugrīva himself was fraught with fear of death at the hands of his brother Vālī and was dependent on Śrī Hanumāna for his protection. How could such a person ever be anyone's true master?

When Śrī Hanumāna saw Lord Rāma for the very first time, he recognized his true master immediately and thereafter, not only did he himself become His loyal and devoted servant, but he also made Sugrīva follow his example. As soon as Sugrīva surrendered at the lotus feet of Lord Rāma, he was blessed and thus received the fruit of his devotion. In Laṅkā also, the she demon Laṅkiṇī and Vibhīṣaṇa were serving Rāvaṇa, the mighty but atrocious king. They were under the notion that they should serve their master, even if he be evil. It is only Śrī Hanumāna who made them realize their mistake. After realising this, they both became devotees of Lord Rāma.

Thus, we see that neither a weak link like Sugrīva nor a mighty person like Rāvaṇa can ever be our true master. Lord

Rāma alone can be a true master. He is great, not because He keeps all beings under His control like Rāvaṇa but because He makes devotees like Śrī Hanumāna greater than Himself.

May we all come to recognize Lord Rāma as our true master and serve Him with the attitude of His great devotee Śrī Hanumāna. May we too like Śrī Hanumāna ever revel in singing the holy name of the Lord – Śrī Rāma jaya Rāma jaya jaya Rāma!

* * *

हनुमान चालीसा

Hanumāna Cālīsā

Om śrī gaṇeśāya namaḥ

Hanumānacālīsā is the most popular composition of the great saint Gosvāmī Tulasīdāsa the author of *Tulasī Rāmāyaṇa*. He composed *Hanumānacālīsā* when he was very sick. It is said that he recovered from his illness when he sang the praise of Śrī Hanumāna. The purpose of singing the glories of the Lord is to purify our speech and mind. It is impossible to describe all His glories because they are infinite. We should chant those of His glories that are dear to us. In the Sundarakāṇḍa of *Tulasī Rāmāyaṇa,* Gosvāmī Tulasīdāsa sings the glory of Śrī Hanumāna:

अतुलितबलधामं हेमशैलाभदेहं
दनुजवनकृशानुं ज्ञानिनामग्रगण्यम् ।
सकलगुणनिधानं वानराणामधीशं
रघुपतिप्रियभक्तं वातजातं नमामि ॥

atulitabaladhāmaṁ hemaśailābhadehaṁ
danujavanakṛśānuṁ jñānināmagragaṇyam,
sakalaguṇanidhānaṁ vānarāṇāmadhīśaṁ
raghupatipriyabhaktaṁ vātajātaṁ namāmi.

'I salute the son of Wind-god, the abode of immeasurable strength, possessing a body shining like a mountain of gold, a fire that consumes the forest of the demon race, the foremost among the wise, a treasure house of every excellence, the chief of the monkeys and Lord Rāma's noble devotee.'

The first thing about Śrī Hanumāna that attracts our attention is his immeasurable and incomparable physical strength coupled with great splendour (tejas). He is resplendent like a golden mountain. It is a rare quality. He uses his strength not to scare ordinary or weak people but to destroy those who give trouble to saintly persons. He not only has physical prowess but is also considered a wise and noble soul (jñānī). His thoughts and words are pure.

The most admirable virtue of Śrī Hanumāna is his humility. Rāvaṇa was strong but he had pride. Such a person does not really command any respect. Śrī Hanumāna was loved and respected by all and was truly the king of all the monkeys. Lord Rāma is very dear to him. Also we can say that Śrī Hanumāna is the favourite devotee of Lord Rāma. When one has love for the Lord, the Lord in turn embraces such a devotee in a thousand ways.

Śrī Hanumāna brought a new life to all. He helped Sugrīva to get rid of his fear of Vālī and he inspired Vibhīṣaṇa to leave the wicked Rāvaṇa and surrender at the feet of the Lord. He saved the life of Mother Sītā, by conveying the message of the Lord to her. He brought the Sanjīvanī plant and saved the life of Lakṣamaṇa. After the war he proceeded back to Ayodhyā, much before Lord Rāma and conveyed the message of the Lord's arrival to Bharata, who was about to immolate himself then.

Hanumānacālīsā talks of the glory of Śrī Hanumāna. It is sung in various parts of India with great love and devotion. Some people chant it as their daily prayer. It is believed that by chanting the *Hanumānacālīsā* seven times or one hundred times our illness, adversity or distress is removed. Some believe Saturday or Tuesday to be a day dedicated to Śrī Hanumāna and they spend the day in thinking about the glories of Śrī Hanumāna, going to the temple and chanting *Hanumānacālīsā*. Thus, we see that this great composition of Gosvāmī Tulasīdāsa has become a part of the culture and religious belief of a large number of people in India. The word cālīsā means forty. This composition has forty verses in praise of Śrī Hanumāna. Those who are familiar with the story of *Rāmāyaṇa* know his greatness. As we read individual verses in detail, we shall appreciate his virtues like love, devotion, service and valour.

In life, it is almost impossible for a person to remain free from blemish. Whether right or wrong, criticisms and accusations are levelled against everyone. None can escape this. Even Lord Rāma and the divine Mother Sītā were not spared. Lord Rāma was an incarnation of righteousness and Mother Sītā, the personification of purity. They were also unfairly blamed and criticized. But there is one character in *Rāmāyaṇa* who is above all criticisms and that is Śrī Hanumāna. He is indeed great as he has remained totally free from all faults and blemish. We shall see this in more detail as we study the text.

* * *

दोहा

श्रीगुरु चरन सरोज रज निज मनु मुकुरु सुधारि ।
बरनउँ रघुबर बिमल जसु जो दायकु फल चारि ॥१॥

dohā

śrīguru carana saroja raja nija manu mukuru sudhāri,
baranauṁ raghubaru bimala jasu jo dāyaku phala cāri. (1)

1. With a spotless (serene) mind, purified by the dust of the lotus feet of Guru, I now (proceed to) describe the unblemished glory of Śrī Hanumāna, the most exalted one of Raghu family, who is capable of bestowing the four results (puruṣārthas) on his devotees.

Hanumānacālīsā is composed in the Avadhi language, which is a dialect of Hindi and is spoken in Ayodhyā (in Uttar Pradesh, India) where Lord Rāma was born. Though an offshoot of Hindi, it has modified over the years. Even students of Hindi may have trouble in understanding certain words of Avadhi. The word baranauṁ means – 'I am going to describe.' It comes from the Sanskrit verb 'varṇa' – to describe. Gosvāmī Tulasīdāsa declares that in these verses he is going to describe the holy, pure and noble glories (bimala jasu) of Raghuvara. Lord Rāma belonged to the dynasty of Raghu (Raghuvaṁśa). Raghu was a great king and the entire dynasty was named after him. Raghuvara means the supreme, the best among the descendants of the Raghu dynasty and usually refers to Lord

Rāma. This particular verse is found in Ayodhyākāṇḍa of *Rāmcarita-mānas*. Therein it refers to the glories of Lord Rāma. In the second half of Ayodhyākāṇḍa, the glories of Bharata (younger brother of Lord Rāma) are extolled. So this verse and the word Raghuvara could also refer to the noble Bharata. Even though *Hanumānacālīsā* indirectly also praises Lord Rāma, it is essentially being sung in praise of Śrī Hanumāna. Why would then, Gosvāmī Tulasīdāsa address Śrī Hanumāna as Raghuvara? As we all know, he was not born in the Raghu dynasty. He was in the form of a monkey. However there is a beautiful meaning to this. *Tulasī Rāmāyaṇa* mentions that he was the adopted son of Lord Rāma and Mother Sītā. When Śrī Hanumāna went to Laṅkā to meet Mother Sītā, she recognized him as a great devotee of Lord Rāma and addressed him as 'suta', my son. In turn Śrī Hanumāna called her as 'jananī' (one who gives birth or mother). When Śrī Hanumāna returned from Laṅkā, Lord Rāma also addressed him as 'son'. Even though Lord Rāma met Śrī Hanumāna first, Mother Sītā was the one who called him her son and developed a motherly relationship with him. In our life also it is the mother who gets close to the child first and the relationship with the father develops later. Thus Śrī Hanumāna, Lord Rāma and Mother Sītā's son, becomes 'one who belongs to the dynasty of Raghu – Raghuvaṁśī'. And because of his noble and divine qualities, he is referred to as Raghuvara, the best amongst the Raghus. However, Śrī Hanumāna gives all the credit for his success to Lord Rāma. In fact, the two are inseparable. Hence this verse describes the glories of both as the descendants of Raghu.

Gosvāmī Tulasīdāsa says, 'I am describing the glories of Śrī Hanumāna.' Śrī Hanumāna was not an ordinary person.

He was not an ordinary king, divine minister or dictator. He is greater than all those. 'Singing his glories gives us all the four goals of life.' The four goals are: dharma, artha, kāma and mokṣa.

Artha refers to wealth and prosperity and kāma means worldly joy or sense pleasures. Some people may be very rich but are not able to enjoy their wealth. They may be so sick that they can't even eat. Their breakfast may be only medicines. Of what use is such wealth? Others may have wealth and enjoy worldly pleasures, but they do not perform any meritorious deeds, dharma. They do not help others and such people suffer in life. Singing the glories of Śrī Hanumāna gives us dharma and also puṇya (merit). But the ultimate goal of human life is liberation from sufferings and from the cycle of birth and death, mokṣa. Śrī Hanumāna can grant this great goal also to us.

How does one prepare oneself to sing the glories of Śrī Hanumāna? It is by purifying one's mind. A clean, pure mind will be able to relate with the Lord and feel His presence everywhere. Gosvāmī Tulasīdāsa says, 'śrīguru caraṇa saroja raja nijamanu mukuru sudhāri.' The word 'sudhāri' signifies perfecting, purifying and cleaning. 'nijamanu mukuru' means the mirror of my mind. 'I will clean the mirror of my mind, so it will reflect the glories of the Lord.' Only in a clean mirror the reflection is clear. 'May the glories of Śrī Hanumāna shine in the mirror of my mind.' How will I clean this mind-mirror? 'guru carana saroja raja'—with the dust of my teacher's lotus feet. By surrendering at the feet of my teacher and serving him, I will be able to cleanse my mind of all impurities.

* * *

दोहा

बुद्धिहीन तनु जानिके, सुमिरौं पवन-कुमार।
बल बुधि बिद्या देहु मोहिं, हरहु कलेस बिकार ॥२॥

dohā

buddhihīna tanu jānike sumiraum̐ pavana-kumāra,
bala budhi bidyā dehu mohim̐ harahu kalesa bikāra. (2)

2. Knowing that I am ignorant, I pray to you (Śrī Hanumāna) the son of Wind-god, to bless me with strength, wisdom and knowledge. Do banish (all) my afflictions.

Sumiraum̐ is derived from the Sanskrit word 'smaraṇa'—to remember. Dialects, at times render sweetness to the difficult Sanskrit words and make them easier to pronounce. The verse says, 'I remember pavana-kumāra, son of the Wind-god; bala budhi bidyā dehu mohim – bless me with strength that includes physical and moral strength and strength of character. Vidyā means knowledge and buddhi is the faculty with which we gain knowledge. If I do not have this faculty, how can I learn or know anything? A blind man has eyes, but does not have sight in the eyes. To gain knowledge, I must have the instrument and ability to know and understand and I must also use it. In this world every man is blessed with an intellect (buddhi) but not every one is intelligent (buddhimāna). A wise man not only learns, but also uses that knowledge for benefitting himself and others. One man was asked, "Why do you always act so foolish, why don't you use your brains?" He said, "God has given me a limited amount of intellect. I have to live for 70 years. If I use it all, right now, it will get depleted. So, I conserve it and use it sparingly!"

People do not use their intellect and this is the reason for bondage and sorrow. Even if they do use it, it is only at a worldly, superficial level. They do not think deeply about themselves, the truth behind this life or this world.

Gosvāmī Tulasīdāsa says, 'Bless me with strength and knowledge.' What will this knowledge do? Harahu kalesa bikāra – this knowledge alone can remove my sufferings. Vikāra means change and that is something which we are afraid of and do not want to accept. Kalesa (in Sanskrit, kleśa) here refers to afflictions and negative tendencies which cause misery. The *Pātañjali Yoga-sūtras* enumerate five kinds of afflictions:

1. Avidyā – ignorance
2. Asmitā – ego
3. Rāgaḥ – likes
4. Dveṣaḥ – dislikes
5. Abhiniveśaḥ – fear of death.

The latter four are products of ignorance and everyone suffers from these five afflictions. The more likes and dislikes we have, the more unhappy we become. If we get the things we like, we are happy and if we get things we dislike, that makes us unhappy. However, it is not always possible to be surrounded by the objects, people and places that we like. Also the things that we like are not permanent and there is always a worry about preserving and multiplying them. All these thoughts increase sorrow and stress. Gosvāmī Tulasīdāsa says that worship of Śrī Hanumāna frees the devotee from all these five afflictions. Buddhihīna tanu jānike – knowing myself to be ignorant. Tanu means body and buddhihīna means ignorant, absence of wisdom. To consider ourselves as the body is ignorance. The body is made of inert matter, has no life and cannot do anything by itself. It is only when this body is enlivened by the Lord and permeated by His power that it comes to life and functions. So people who give importance only to this body and ignore the Lord are not very wise (buddhihīna).

To summarize, first we must cleanse our mind by serving our teacher. Once our mind is clean, the glories of the Lord will shine clearly in our heart. With this attitude, thereafter we sing the glories of the Lord and we shall get all that we seek, noble virtues (dharma), prosperity (artha), pleasures (kāma) and liberation (mokṣa). All our sorrows will end and our ignorance will vanish. A powerful prayer indeed!

Śrī Hanumāna (Pavana-kumāra), was the son of the Wind-god. The wind keeps on blowing and therefore it is a great purifier. A room that has all windows and doors shut after a while becomes very stuffy. The moment we open the windows, the fresh air blows in and purifies the atmosphere. So the Wind-god is considered a great purifier. His son, Śrī Hanumāna also moves around from place to place and wherever he goes, he purifies the atmosphere. People who come in contact with him also get purified. Also the wind always serves us silently. The sun serves us during the day and the moon illumines the earth at night. We see them when they are present and notice their absence when they are not visible. However, the wind serves us both day and night. It is within us in the form of vital air (prāṇa) and without it, we would be dead. We do not see the wind and it serves us silently without any pomp or show. Hence, we often take it for granted. The wind does not have any ego and serves us selflessly.

Similarly, Pavana-kumāra, Śrī Hanumāna served Lord Rāma like the wind throughout his life. He has no sense of pride, arrogance or false ego. His goal is to serve the Lord. He did so with humility and devotion. These are qualities that we need to imbibe in us. Let us always serve others silently, humbly and devotedly without expecting any praise or reward.

* * *

चौपाई

जय हनुमान ज्ञान गुन सागर।
जय कपीस तिहुँ लोक उजागर ॥१॥

jaya hanumāna jñāna guna sāgara,
jaya kapīsa tihuṁ loka ujāgara. (1)

1. Victory to you, O Hanumāna, who is an ocean of knowledge and virtues. Victory to you, O Lord of the monkeys, who is well known in all the three worlds.

Hanu means chin. Hanumāna means one with chin. Then everyone with a chin can be called Hanumāna! Śrī Hanumāna's chin was cut or cleaved in the middle and his mouth appeared swollen. How did this happen? He was born at dawn. As soon as he was born, he saw the rising sun and thought it was a ripe fruit. He was born with the ability to fly and he flew to the sun and swallowed it. The whole world became dark. Nobody could fathom how this little child had swallowed the sun.

At that time, Lord Indra, king of all deities, arrived with his thunderbolt. His thunderbolt is infallible and whoever is struck by it dies instantly. To release the sun, Lord Indra struck that little child with his thunderbolt. The thunderbolt struck Śrī Hanumāna on the chin. However, being all-powerful, he did not die but the sun was released and he fell on the earth and became unconscious. When the Wind-god came to know what had happened, he was very angry and stopped the flow of air. Everyone panicked without air. They started praying to the Wind-god and all deities came and sought his apology. The Wind-god said, "All of you will have to bless my son with all your powers and the virtues that you possess." They agreed to do so and thus Śrī Hanumāna came to be blessed with all might and strength.

Śrī Hanumāna is so strong that he could withstand a blow from the mighty thunderbolt of Lord Indra. Gosvāmī Tulasīdāsa says that Śrī Hanumāna is strong and he uses this strength to serve the Lord and others. Many who are strong, use their strength to subjugate others and become dictators. Śrī Hanumāna does not misuse his strength.

Jñāna guna sāgara means an ocean of knowledge and virtue. Often, people with some knowledge or a university degree become very arrogant. They consider themselves superior to others. But Śrī Hanumāna's knowledge is coupled with noble virtues and so he is the best among all learned people (buddhimatāṁ variṣṭham). The greatest virtues are humility and nobility of character. He is the very embodiment of these virtues. And the greatest knowledge is Self-knowledge. Śrī Hanumāna has that as well. Lord Rāma once asked him, "What is your relationship with me?" Śrī Hanumāna answered, "With reference to my body, I am your servant, as an individual soul, I am a part of You (and You are the Whole) but as the Self, we both are one. This is my firm conviction."[1]

Besides, Śrī Hanumāna is always good in his dealings with everyone and dealt with each person appropriately – according

---

[1] *deha-buddhyā tu dāso'smi jīva-buddhyā tvadaṁśakaḥ,*
ātma-buddhyā tvamevāham iti me niścitā matiḥ. – Vālmīki Rāmāyaṇa

to his rank and stature. *Vālmīki Rāmāyaṇa* says that he was a scholar and knew the nine kinds of Sanskrit grammar (nava-vyākaraṇa paṇḍitaḥ). Even with such abounding knowledge he is an epitome of humility (guna sāgara). Jaya kapīsa means victory to the Lord of the monkeys. Kapī means monkey and īsa means Lord. He was not the king of monkeys then why is he called kapīsa? Initially Vālī was the king of the monkeys and later Sugrīva. They were kings, but Śrī Hanumāna was the kingmaker, hence the Lord. Being afraid of his brother, when Sugrīva was running around, it was Śrī Hanumāna's courage and bravery that gave him strength. And who is a true king? Is it one who rules over some land or a kingdom, one who inherits power, one who gets voted to power by the majority or is it one who rules over the hearts of all? A crowned king is one who is coronated by his subjects but true lordship is worshipped and respected by all even if it be an uncrowned person. Śrī Hanumāna was indeed the uncrowned king of the monkeys.

Also the word 'kapī' stands for one who drinks the joy of the Truth (Brahman) which alone is true happiness. 'Ka' – joy (sukham) and 'pī' – one who drinks (pibati). The *Chāndogyopaniṣad* says, 'That which is infinite alone is happiness. There is no happiness in finitude.' So one who knows this and revels in the joy of Truth is a kapī. Śrī Hanumāna is not an ordinary monkey and we should not insult him by calling him a monkey-god. He may be in the form of a monkey, but he is a brahmajñānī, one who has supreme Knowledge.

Tihuṁ loka ujāgara means he who is well known in all the three worlds. The light of his fame spreads everywhere, everyone knows him and respects him.

* * *

राम दूत अतुलित बल धामा।
अंजनि-पुत्र पवनसुत नामा ॥२॥

rāma dūta atulita bala dhāmā,
añjani-putra pavanasuta nāmā. (2)

2. You are the envoy of Lord Rāma, an abode of incomparable strength, the son of Añjanī, popularly known by the name Pavana-suta (son of the Wind-god).

Śrī Hanumāna is a messenger of Lord Rāma. The job of a messenger is difficult. One has to make sure that one delivers the message promptly and correctly. In Śrī Hanumāna's case, the job was more difficult because he had to deliver a message to the enemy, king Rāvaṇa of Laṅkā. He could even get killed in this endeavour. He also had to secretly deliver Lord Rāma's message to Mother Sītā, concealing himself from all the demon guards. But Śrī Hanumāna's greatness is that whatever h undertakes, he does well, with complete devotion and courage

He is the very epitome of immeasurable and incomparabl (atulita) strength. The first thing that one notices about Śrī Hanumāna is his superhuman power. His mother's name was Añjani (or Añjanā), which means pure intellect. So, he was born of pure intellect, the son of a pure hearted mother. Añjana also means the beautifying and sight enhancing paste that one puts in one's eyes. The grace of the Master (guru-kṛpā) is considered as the 'añjana' by which one realises the whole world to be Lord Rāma.

The word 'putra' means one who saves his parents from going to hell[1]. Various kinds of heavens and hells are described in our scriptures. One of these is called 'puṁ'. A true son is one who protects his parents from suffering and misery. Such a son was Śrī Hanumāna. He protected his parents and also brought much fame to his parents. If not for him, who would have known Añjani?

1 puṁ nāma narakāt trāyate iti putra

* * *

महाबीर बिक्रम बजरंगी ।
कुमति निवार सुमति के संगी ॥३॥

mahābīra bikrama bajaraṅgī,
kumati nivāra sumati ke saṅgī. (3)

3. With a body as strong as a thunderbolt, you are a great warrior of incomparable valour. Do remove my wicked thoughts and grant me the company of the wise.

'Vīra' is a man of courage, strength and valour. Śrī Hanumāna is a 'mahābīra', the greatest warrior. Lord Rāma Himself sang his glories. Some people, poets or writers may glorify a brave warrior. But when the Lord Himself honours and praises a person, that person cannot be an ordinary one.

Generally vīra refers to one who displays heroism and courage on the battlefield. But there are five kinds of heroism (vīratā) mentioned in the scriptures:

1. Tyāgavīra or dharmavīra – Heroism in renunciation and sacrifice. One often has to sacrifice for the sake of righteousness. One who does so to live a life of dharma is called tyāgavīra.

2. Dayāvīra – Heroism in compassion. One who cannot bear the sorrows of others and will do his/her best to alleviate them is dayāvīra.

3. Vidyāvīra – Heroism in knowledge and learning.

4. Dānavīra – Heroism in charity. Śrī Hanumāna gives you anything you seek – dharma, artha, kāma or mokṣa. But the greatest gift he can bestow is devotion to Lord Rāma (Rāma-bhakti).

5. Raṇavīra – Bravery on the battlefield.

In the world, we may find people who have one of the five kinds of heroism. One may be brave in battle, but may lack knowledge (vidyā) or compassion (dayā). Śrī Hanumāna has all five kinds of valour, hence he is called mahābīra. If all the five are used to serve the Lord, there can be nothing greater. Such a person is called a supreme Hero (paramavīra). Lord Rāma felt grateful towards Śrī Hanumāna who served Him in all ways and so He said, "I am forever indebted to you. I will never be able to repay you." Bikrama also means a mighty person, who has great valour.

Śrī Hanumāna is also known as bajaraṅgī. The original Sanskrit word is vajra-aṅgī. The word vajra-aṅgī became bajaraṅgī in Avadhi language, which is easier to pronounce. Śrī Hanumāna has a body, strong enough to withstand the thunderbolt of Lord Indra.

Kumati nivāra sumati ke saṅgī – 'Kumati' means all vicious or negative tendencies of the mind. 'Nivāra' means to get rid of. Do eliminate all illusions of the mind. 'Sumati ke saṅgī' means do give us bright intellect or you are the friend of a person of good intellect. Śrī Hanumāna gives us good thoughts and eliminates evil thoughts. These words can also mean that Śrī Hanumāna punishes people who are evil and he supports those who are good.

* * *

कंचन बरन बिराज सुबेसा ।
कानन कुंडल कुंचित केसा ॥४ ॥

kañcana barana birāja subesā,
kānana kuṇḍala kuñcita kesā. (4)

4. Your golden complexion shines with the attractive clothes (which you are wearing), with the glittering earrings and (your) curly hair.

हाथ बज्र औ ध्वजा बिराजै ।
काँधे मूँज जनेऊ साजै ॥५ ॥

hātha bajra au dhvajā birājai,
kām̐dhe mūm̐ja janeū sājai. (5)

5. You have the thunderbolt (in one hand) and the flag (in another) and the sacred thread across your shoulder made of mūm̐ja grass decorates you.

Śrī Hanumāna carries a mace (gadā) in his hand which is as strong as Lord Indra's thunderbolt and kills whoever it is used on. The word 'gadā' comes from 'gada' which means 'to speak.' This weapon is used to eliminate enemies in the battlefield and also to destroy ignorance and ego with the help of words (true knowledge). Dhvajā birājai means he carries the flag of Lord Rāma in his hand which symbolically shows that he always honours and remembers Lord Rāma. Dhvajā also stands for victory. He always declares victory of Lord Rāma. Usually flags were flown on chariots in the battlefield to identify them as a friend or a foe. Śrī Hanumāna's body itself is like a chariot that flies from place to place. He thus carries Lord Rāma's flag in his hand to declare his glory and victory. Gosvāmī Tulasīdāsa says that Śrī Hanumāna carries the flag of truthfulness, good character and faith in God's name.

Kāṁdhe mūṁja janeū sājai – Janeū is the sacred thread made of cotton that is worn over one shoulder when one is initiated into Gāyatrī-mantra. Originally it used to be made of mūṁjā grass and therefore known as mūṁjā janeū. The thread ceremony is carried out, when a boy is between 5 and 10 years of age. It signifies that his playful childhood days are over. Thereafter, he has to begin a life of study and discipline. The knot in the thread represents Brahman—the supreme Consciousness. The three threads woven together represent the three qualities (sattva, rajas and tamas). These three qualities are centered on Brahman. Traditionally, people are advised to hold on to the knot while chanting the Gāyatrī-mantra. Śrī Hanumāna wears the sacred thread made of mūṁjā grass on his shoulder and his attention is always on the Truth (Brahman).

* * *

संकर सुवन केसरीनंदन ।
तेज प्रताप महा जग बंदन ॥६॥

saṅkara suvana kesarīnandana,
teja pratāpa mahā jaga bandana. (6)

6. You are the son of Śiva and also of Kesarī. Everyone in the world respects you because of your lustre and great valour.

Saṅkara suvana Kesarī-nandana – Son of Lord Śiva and also of Kesarī. One may wonder how many people is he the son of – Wind-god, Lord Śiva and Kesarī? When Rāvaṇa's atrocities were increasing and he was playing havoc in the world, all the deities and ascetics prayed to Lord Viṣṇu. They told Him that the earth could not take any more misery caused by Rāvaṇa and requested the Lord to come and save everyone. The Lord said, "I will take birth as Rāma, to free the earth from the evil grip of Rāvaṇa". Lord Brahmā said to all the gods, "Since Lord Viṣṇu is coming to this earth, we must all serve Him. As He is manifesting in the human form (nara), we should all assume a form lower than a nara, so we should become monkeys (vānara)." So, all the monkeys that served Lord Rāma were none other than the gods themselves. Vālī was the son of Indra, Sugrīva was the son of Sūrya and so on. Vāyu blessed Añjani and Kesarī (parents of Śrī Hanumāna) with his glow (tejas). This power was placed in Śrī Hanumāna when he was born. Therefore he is called the son of Wind-god.

Lord Śiva and Lord Viṣṇu are good friends. When one takes birth, the other wants to serve him. Lord Śiva thought,

"I wish to serve Lord Viṣṇu when He comes as Lord Rāma. If I become a part of His family, He may hesitate to be served by me and may want to serve me instead. But if I assume a lower form - that of a monkey, there will be no such problem." Thinking thus, he placed his tejas in Śrī Hanumāna in order to serve Lord Rāma. Therefore, Śrī Hanumāna is known as the son of Lord Śiva (saṅkara suvana) and also known as an incarnation of Lord Śiva (rudra avatāra).

His father's name was Kesarī, which also means 'lion'. Śrī Hanumāna is born of a lion-like father who is fearless, brave and strong. Śrī Hanumāna has imbibed these virtues from him. He also purifies everything that comes in contact with him, like the Wind-god and blesses everyone, like Lord Śiva. Thus, he is a worthy son of all three.

Teja pratāpa mahā jaga bandana – His glow or fame is very great and is praised by the entire world. Everyone sings the glory of Śrī Hanumāna.

* * *

बिद्यावान गुनी अति चातुर।
राम काज करिबे को आतुर॥७॥

bidyāvāna gunī ati cātura,
rāma kāja karibe ko ātura. (7)

7. You are full of knowledge and virtues and are highly intelligent. You are ever ready to carry out the work of Lord Rāma.

Bidyāvāna – Man of great knowledge. Gunī – A person of great virtue. Ati cātura – Extremely wise. There are many people in this world who are very energetic and wise but all their energy is directed into worldly matters. If you ask them to do anything of a spiritual nature or for others like going to a temple or giving in charity, they suddenly find all kinds of excuses. They will wake up early in the morning to play tennis, not for meditation. But Śrī Hanumāna is ever ready to do the Lord's work. When Lakṣamaṇa was shot by the arrow of Indrajit (Rāvaṇa's son), he fell unconscious. The life-saving Sañjīvanī plant (a kind of elixir) had to be brought immediately to save his life. Śrī Hanumāna said, "I will be back with the plant in the time that it takes the mustard seeds to cook when put in boiling hot oil." When he went to the Himalayan mountains, he could not find the plant so he brought the entire mountain. He serves continuously with all readiness, alertness, dedication and devotion (rāma kāja karibe ko ātura).

* * *

प्रभु चरित्र सुनिबे को रसिया।
राम लषन सीता मन बसिया ॥८॥

prabhu caritra sunibe ko rasiyā,
rāma laṣana sītā mana basiyā. (8)

8. You (always take) delight in listening to the glories of the Lord. Lord Rāma, Lakṣamaṇa and Mother Sītā always reside in your heart.

Śrī Hanumāna is delighted (rasiyā) in listening to the glories of the Lord. Usually, this is not our nature. When a man becomes famous, he wants people to talk about his glory. He does not want to listen to the glories of others. He does not even want to talk about the Lord's glories. But Śrī Hanumāna always revels in speaking about the Lord and is eager to hear others speaking about the virtues of Lord Rāma.

Lord Rāma, Lakṣamaṇa and Mother Sītā always dwell in his heart. It also means that Śrī Hanumāna lives in their heart. Lord Rāma represents Self-knowledge (jñāna), Mother Sītā represents devotion (bhakti) and Lakṣamaṇa stands for sacrifice (tyāga) and dispassion (vairāgya). Śrī Hanumāna has all of them – knowledge, devotion, sacrifice and dispassion.

* * *

सुक्ष्म रूप धरि सियहिं दिखावा ।
बिकट रूप धरि लंक जरावा ॥९॥

sukṣma rūpa dhari siyahiṁ dikhāvā,
bikaṭa rūpa dhari laṅka jarāvā. (9)

9. You assumed a tiny form when you revealed yourself to Mother Sītā and a fierce form to burn down (the city of) Laṅkā .

Śrī Hanumāna had the power to become small or big at will. When he went to meet Mother Sītā, he became as small as an insect so he could approach her without being detected by the guards. In general, people who are big do not want to become small. Their pride prevents them from doing simple and ordinary things before others. But Śrī Hanumāna has no such ego. He does whatever is required to accomplish the Lord's work, which to him is all important.

He assumed a huge form to burn down Rāvaṇa's Laṅkā . This has several meanings. He destroyed Rāvaṇa's palaces and forts. Laṅkā represents pleasures, material possessions and an indulgent life. During that time the people, who lived there, were mostly demons (asuras). Thinking themselves to be only the body, they did everything for bodily comforts and enjoyment. So, he destroyed the land of sensuality. He also had the right knowledge that, 'I am not this body and life is not meant only to pamper the body and indulge in pleasures and comforts.' This fire of Self-knowledge kindled by Śrī Hanumāna burnt down the wrong lifestyle, false notions, body identification and attachments. Another fire is the fire of Mother Sītā's sorrow. It is said that when noble people are tortured, their suffering destroys those who trouble them. The fire of Mother Sītā's sorrow burnt Laṅkā to ashes.

* * *

भीम रूप धरि असुर सँहारे।
रामचन्द्र के काज सँवारे ॥१० ॥

bhīma rūpa dhari asura saṁhāre,
rāmacandra ke kāja saṁvāre. (10)

10. Assuming a dreadful form to destroy the demons, you accomplished the mission of Lord Rāma.

लाय सजीवन लखन जियाये।
श्रीरघुबीर हरषि उर लाये ॥११ ॥

lāya sajīvana lakhana jiyāye,
śrīraghubīra haraṣi uru lāye. (11)

11. You fetched Sañjīvanī to revive Lakṣamaṇa (who had fainted on the battlefield) which made Lord Rāma embrace you with joy.

The arrow of Indrajit struck Lakṣamaṇa and Śrī Hanumāna brought the life saving Sañjīvanī plant that brought him back to life. Lord Rāma was so delighted by this act that he embraced Śrī Hanumāna. It is evident that when the Lord embraces His devotee, He places His heart in the devotee's heart. So, if you want to find the Lord, you have to search for Him in the heart of a true devotee.

* * *

रघुपति कीन्ही बहुत बड़ाई ।
तुम मम प्रिय भरतहि सम भाई ॥१२ ॥

raghupati kīnhī bahuta baḍāī,
tuma mama priya bharatahi sama bhāī. (12)

12. Lord Rāma praised (you) very highly (and said), "You are as dear to me as my brother Bharata."

सहस बदन तुम्हरो जस गावैं ।
अस कहि श्रीपति कण्ठ लगावैं ॥१३ ॥

sahasa badana tumharo jasa gāvaiṁ,
asa kahi śrīpati kaṇṭha lagāvaiṁ. (13)

13. Embracing him, Lord Rāma said, "Even Śeṣa, the thousand-headed serpent sings your glory."

It is believed that everyone meditates on Lord Rāma, but He meditates on Bharata, His younger brother, who was very dear to Him. Lord Rāma says, "I love you as much as my dear brother Bharata, whom I remember at all times with great love".

Gosvāmī Tulasīdāsa says – Sahasa badana tumharo jasa gāvaiṁ – The thousand-headed snake (Śeṣa) is singing your glories, but even thousand mouths are not enough to sing your glories. Secondly, Śeṣa himself incarnated as Lakṣamaṇa and he always sang Śrī Hanumāna's glories.

Asa kahi Śrīpati kaṇṭha lagāvai – Śrīpati or Lakṣmīpati refers to Lord Rāma (Lakṣmī is Lord Viṣṇu's consort). He embraced Śrī Hanumāna and praised him.

* * *

सनकादिक ब्रह्मादि मुनीसा।
नारद सारद सहित अहीसा॥१४॥

sanakādika brahmādi munīsā,
nārada sārada sahita ahīsā. (14)

14. The (great) sages like Sanaka, Nārada and others and gods like Brahmā, Śeṣa (the King of Serpents) and goddess Śāradā,

जम कुबेर दिगपाल जहाँ ते।
कबि कोबिद कहि सके कहाँ ते॥१५॥

jama kubera digapāla jahām̐ te,
kabi kobida kahi sake kahām̐ te. (15)

15. Yama – the God of death, Kubera – the God of wealth, the eight guardians of the directions, poets and scholars have not been able to praise you adequately.

The Sanatkumāras, Brahmā, Indra, Vāyu, Kubera (all the Gods) and sages also praise you. The great sages like Nārada, Śāradā (Sarasvatī – Goddess of Knowledge) all sing your glories. Yama – God of Death, Kubera –treasurer of Gods, Dik-pālakas – guardians of all the directions, great poets, scholars, puṇḍits – all praise you and sing your glories. Gosvāmī Tulasīdāsa says, 'Your virtues are innumerable, how long can we enumerate them?'

* * *

तुम उपकार सुग्रीवहिं कीन्हा।
राम मिलाय राज पद दीन्हा ॥१६॥

tuma upakāra sugrīvahiṁ kīnhā,
rāma milāya rāja pada dīnhā. (16)

16. You helped Sugrīva in regaining his kingdom by making him meet Lord Rāma.

Sugrīva was the king of monkeys. His brother Vālī (also known as Bālī) drove him out of the kingdom and became the king. He kept trying to kill Sugrīva who lived on the Ṛṣyamūka mountain. When Sugrīva saw Lord Rāma and Lakṣamaṇa approaching, he was afraid and thought that they were sent by Bālī to kill him. They looked so brave and strong that he started running away from them. At that time Śrī Hanumāna said, "Why don't you find out who they are, before running away? Don't assume that they are your enemies." Thus giving him courage, Śrī Hanumāna brought Lord Rāma to Sugrīva and forged a friendship between them. Lord Rāma then killed Bālī and Sugrīva was crowned the king of Kiṣkindhā. The Lord is the supreme Truth. By introducing Lord Rāma to Sugrīva, Śrī Hanumāna gave him the knowledge of supreme Truth. Śrī Hanumāna expects nothing for himself and he always remains as a servant of the Lord. This is his greatness.

* * *

तुम्हरो मन्त्र बिभीषन माना ।
लंकेस्वर भए सब जग जाना ॥१७ ॥

tumharo mantra bibhīṣana mānā,
laṅkesvara bhae saba jaga jānā. (17)

17. Vibhīṣaṇa heeded to your advice. The entire world knows that he became the king of Laṅkā.

Here, mantra means advice (mantraṇā). Śrī Hanumāna advised Vibhīṣaṇa (Rāvaṇa's brother) to surrender to Lord Rāma. No sooner did Vibhīṣaṇa do that, Lord Rāma appointed him as the King of Laṅkā. Lord Rāma never asked either Sugrīva or Vibhīṣaṇa to fulfil his task in return for crowning them as kings. All they had to do was to surrender to the Lord and all glory was theirs. This shows that, by surrendering to Lord Rāma, we get both material and spiritual powers.

* * *

जुग सहस्त्र जोजन पर भानु ।
लील्यो ताहि मधुर फल जानू ॥१८ ॥

juga sahasra jojana para bhānu,
līlyo tāhi madhura phala jānū. (18)

18. You leaped quite easily at the Sun (who is) thousands of miles away thinking it to be a sweet fruit.

When Śrī Hanumāna was born, he saw the sun in the sky. Thinking it to be a fruit, he flew towards it and swallowed it. Some people say that this is impossible. But he is the son of Wind-god. The sun is fire and wind (vāyu) is the cause of fire. After all, fire merges into the air. So, why can't air swallow fire? This is a principle of Vedānta. Further, Śrī Hanumāna is not an ordinary monkey. So we need not doubt his powers. He had all the powers that ascetics (yogīs) and deities have. He had the eight-fold powers (aṣṭasiddhis) about which we shall see in a later verse. One more explanation for this is that, a child's mind is always pure and a child's imagination runs very high. He always asks questions about the sun, the moon and the stars. How does it rain? Where did I come from? He does not ask questions about power and money until he grows up. So, a child's imagination flies to the sun. Adults do not want to answer the child's questions and ask him to shut up. Similarly, Lord Indra (a typical adult) struck Śrī Hanumāna with his thunderbolt (words) so that he would not fly high (shut up). That is why according to the story, the world became dark until Śrī Hanumāna released the sun.

* * *

प्रभु मुद्रिका मेलि मुख माहीं।
जलधि लाँघि गये अचरज नाहीं ॥१९॥

prabhu mudrikā meli mukha māhīṁ,
jaladhi lām̐ghi gaye acaraja nāhīṁ. (19)

19. Holding the Lord's (Rāma's) ring in your mouth, you flew over (crossed) the ocean, which is no wonder (as you are capable of any achievement).

The monkeys were sent in search of Mother Sītā. They came to the vast ocean. On the other side was Laṅkā. They did not know how to cross the ocean. Śrī Hanumāna put Lord Rāma's ring in his mouth. By the strength and power of His name, he was able to cross the vast ocean and reach Laṅkā. Great indeed is the power of the Lord's name. Also, Mother Sītā represents devotion (bhakti) and to reach devotion or liberation (mokṣa) you have to cross an ocean. What is this ocean? – the notion that 'I am this body' (dehātmabhāva). This false notion is as difficult to overcome as crossing an ocean. But by chanting the Lord's name, we purify our mind and come to understand that we are not this body and in this way, we cross this ocean of saṁsāra (worldliness). There is no doubt (acaraja nāhīṁ) that one can accomplish anything by chanting the Lord's name with full faith and devotion. People with such faith are not afraid of anything in this world.

* * *

दुर्गम काज जगत के जेते ।
सुगम अनुग्रह तुम्हरे तेते ॥२० ॥

durgama kāja jagata ke jete,
sugama anugraha tumhare tete. (20)

20. By your grace even the most difficult of tasks become easy to accomplish.

Whatever difficulties or obstacles we encounter in life, we are able to overcome them by the grace of Śrī Hanumāna. There are three kinds of people in this world.

1. Those who do not start any new projects or tasks for fear of obstacles. They keep on imagining all kinds of problems and obstacles, hence they never get started.

2. Those who start a lot of projects, but the moment they encounter difficulty or resistance, they become dejected or lose patience and quit or move to another project. They too do not get the satisfaction of accomplishment.

3. Those who, when they encounter obstacles, become more enthusiastic and courageous. Such people do not quit until their work is finished. They gain true fulfilment and success.

Śrī Hanumāna blesses the third type of people and makes their job easier. Even the most difficult task becomes easy to accomplish.

* * *

राम दुआरे तुम रखवारे ।
होत न आज्ञा बिनु पैसारे ॥२१ ॥

rāma duāre tuma rakhavāre,
hota na ājñā binu paisāre. (21)

21. You guard the door (entry) to Lord Rāma's palace where none dare enter (or go out) without your permission.

सब सुख लहै तुम्हारी सरना ।
तुम रच्छक काहू को डर ना ॥२२ ॥

saba sukha lahai tumhārī saranā
tuma racchaka kāhū ko ḍara nā . (22)

22. All those who seek refuge in you enjoy every kind of happiness. Why should one be afraid of anything when you are there to protect?

Śrī Hanumāna is the ever vigilant guard at the door of Śrī Rāma. That does not mean that he will prevent us from entering. On the contrary, he draws people towards Lord Rāma. That is his job. Due to this very reason, Śrī Hanumāna is dearer to Lord Rāma than even Lakṣamaṇa. Lord Rāma said, "By his devotion Śrī Hanumāna inspires other people to love Me and come towards Me."

Earlier it was said : tuma upakāra sugrīvahiṁ kīnhā, tumharo mantra bibhīṣana mānā – With the help of

Śrī Hanumāna, Sugrīva regained his kingdom and Vibhīṣaṇa listened to his advice and took refuge in Lord Rāma.

Not only can we accomplish everything by taking Lord Rāma's name, but we can accomplish anything even by chanting Śrī Hanumāna's name. He makes us brave and fearless, and fills us with devotion, faith and strength. Surrender to Śrī Hanumāna and we will get all his qualities. Also, Śrī Hanumāna will take us to Lord Rāma (the Lord Himself) which is the greatest goal for all human beings.

* * *

आपन तेज सम्हारो आपै ।
तीनों लोक हाँक तें काँपै ॥२३ ॥

āpana teja samhāro āpai,
tīnoṁ loka hāṁka teṁ kāṁpai. (23)

23. You alone are capable of controlling your power. All the three worlds tremble when you roar.

भूत पिसाच निकट नहिं आवै ।
महाबीर जब नाम सुनावै ॥२४ ॥

bhūta pisāca nikaṭa nahim āvai,
mahābīra jaba nāma sunāvai. (24)

24. Evil spirits dare not go near a person on hearing the name of the great warrior (Śrī Hanumāna) being repeated.

Śrī Hanumāna's power is so great that no one can gain control over him. When his mighty roar is heard, all the three worlds (heaven, earth and the netherworlds) tremble in fear. His power and strength know no limits. Chanting the name of Śrī Hanumāna transfers the same power and courage to his devotee. Ghosts and demons do not come near such a person.

What are ghosts? It is believed that if a person suffers an untimely death (due to murder or suicide) then his spirit haunts that place. Normally after death, the soul takes up another body. But if for some reason, it does not happen immediately, then that spirit stays around for a while and that is called a ghost. Chanting Śrī Hanumāna's name will keep all ghosts and evil spirits away from us.

* * *

नासै रोग हरै सब पीरा ।
जपत निरंतर हनुमत बीरा ॥२५॥

nāsai roga harai saba pīrā,
japata nirantara hanumata bīrā. (25)

25. All the ailments, diseases and afflictions vanish when your name is repeated continuously.

For one who constantly chants the name of Śrī Hanumāna, his/her diseases are cured and his/her pains are taken away. Even incurable diseases can be cured. Someone may ask, "If I have cancer, can it be cured?" Yes. If you have complete faith, that too is possible. However, all diseases we suffer from, are diseases of the body and the mind. Diseases of the body are known in Sanskrit as vyādhi and of the mind, ādhi. These cause suffering only if we think that we are this body and mind. But if we falsify this body-mind identification and related attachments, then we will not be afraid even to die. We will accept diseases of the body and mind with more grace and courage and they will not affect us. Śrī Hanumāna takes us to Lord Rāma; he makes us realize that the Lord and the Self are one in essence. To such a person, bodily and mental afflictions no longer exist. They have transcended all sorrow.

* * *

संकट तें हनुमान छुड़ावै।
मन क्रम बचन ध्यान जो लावै ॥२६॥

saṅkaṭa teṁ hanumāna chuḍāvai,
mana krama bacana dhyāna jo lāvai. (26)

26. Śrī Hanumāna helps overcome all difficulties of those who worship him (sincere and with faith) with thoughts, actions, words and prayers.

If we worship Śrī Hanumāna in thought, word and deed, he will free us from all difficulties. Mana is mind, krama (karma) is deed and bacana (vacana) is words. So all our thoughts, words and actions should be a worship of the Lord, then no actions will bind us or cause any sorrow.

* * *

सब पर राम तपस्वी राजा।
तिन के काज सकल तुम साजा ॥२७॥

saba para rāma tapasvī rājā,
tina ke kāja sakala tuma sājā. (27)

27. You carried out all the tasks of Lord Rāma who is a supreme ascetic ruling over everyone.

और मनोरथ जो कोइ लावै।
सोइ अमित जीवन फल पावै ॥२८॥

aura manoratha jo koi lāvai,
soi amita jīvana phala pāvai. (28)

28. You bless everyone who seeks Your grace and grant them in large measure all they want and also grant them the fruit of long life.

If we worship Śrī Hanumāna, all our jobs will be accomplished and we will never be unsuccessful. What is the guarantee? Think of it. Śrī Hanumāna was able to accomplish all the tasks assigned to him by Lord Rāma Himself. So, if he can carry out the Lord's tasks, why can't he accomplish ours? And whatever we desire in life, Śrī Hanumāna will grant us. He will do anything for us. However, we should see that our desires are noble.

* * *

चारों जुग परताप तुम्हारा ।
है परसिद्ध जगत उजियारा ॥२९ ॥

cāroṁ juga paratāpa tumhārā,
hai parasiddha jagata ujiyārā. (29)

29. Your glory radiates through all the four yugas and Your fame shines everywhere in the universe.

साधु संत के तुम रखवारे ।
असुर निकंदन राम दुलारे ॥३० ॥

sādhu santa ke tuma rakhavāre,
asura nikandana rāma dulāre. (30)

30. You are the protector of the righteous and destroyer of the wicked. You are very dear to Lord Rāma.

Your fame is prevalent in all the four ages (yugas – Satya, Tretā, Dvāpara and Kali). Śrī Hanumāna was here on this earth when Lord Rāma incarnated in Tretāyuga. Then how could his glory be present in all four ages? The Lord's glory is eternal and His devotee's glory is also eternal. Secondly, the four ages follow each other in a cycle. Kaliyuga is followed again by Satyayuga. So, Śrī Hanumāna's glory will be remembered forever. And besides that, the Wind-god is always present and without him life is not possible. So his son Śrī Hanumāna is also (cirañjīvī), one who lives forever.

He is the protector of the saints and sages and destroyer of demons. So, if a person is mighty, he should use his strength to help good people and combat wicked ones. No wonder Śrī Hanumāna is so dear to Lord Rāma!

* * *

अष्ट सिद्धि नौ निधि के दाता ।
असि बर दीन जानकी माता ॥३१॥

aṣṭa siddhi nau nidhi ke dātā,
asa bara dīna jānakī mātā. (31)

31. Jānakīmātā (Mother Sītā) bestowed on you the boon that you may grant the eight siddhis (supernatural powers) and the nine forms of wealth to anyone you like.

When Śrī Hanumāna went to Laṅkā to meet Mother Sītā, he saw her and gave her the news of Lord Rāma and sang His glories. Prior to this, Mother Sītā was very unhappy, but as soon as she heard that Lord Rāma was coming to take her back, her joy knew no bounds. She immediately blessed Śrī Hanumāna, saying, "You will be the giver of the eight-fold supernatural powers of Yogīs (aṣṭa siddhi) and nine kinds of wealth of Kubera (navanidhi)."

The eight-fold supernatural powers described in the scriptures are :

1. Aṇimā – The power to assume a very small form (like an atomic particle) or to become so subtle that one can pervade even the smallest particle in the universe.

2. Mahimā – The power to become large, to pervade everything – from the smallest to the largest object. When Śrī Hanumāna went to Laṅkā, he became as small as a mosquito whilst meeting Mother Sītā and became huge whilst confronting the demons.

3. Garimā – The power to make oneself heavy. Even a limb of the body becomes so heavy that no one can lift it. There is a story that once the mighty warrior Bhīma of *Mahābhārata* fame was walking in the forest. He encountered Śrī Hanumāna lying on the side of the path with his long tail across the path. Thinking him to be an ordinary old monkey, Bhīma asked Śrī Hanumāna to remove his tail from the path. Śrī Hanumāna said, "I am old, why don't you lift my tail and remove it?" Bhīma tried to lift it, but despite all his strength, he was unable to move it even an inch. That was when he realized that this was no ordinary monkey and prostrated before him in humility. Here Śrī Hanumāna displayed the garimā siddhi that he had.

4. Laghimā – The power to become light like a feather. When he was in Laṅkā, Śrī Hanumāna was huge, taller than the tallest palace. But still, he was able to jump lightly from rooftop to rooftop, without crushing the buildings. This is due to laghimā siddhi.

5. Prāpti – The power to attain whatever one desires. With this power one is able to sit in one place and watch everything that is going on not only on this earth, but also in other worlds like Brahmaloka. With television satellites and telescopes one is able to see part of this cosmos. One with the power of prāpti can see and experience everything in all the entire cosmoses.

6. Prākāmya or Prākāśya – Prākāmya is the ability to go anywhere in the three worlds – earth, heavens and netherworlds.

Prākāśya is to have a self-illuminating, shining body. Śrī Kṛṣṇa's body was like that. When the Gopīs hid the butter in a dark place, He would come at night with His friends and because of His luminous body, they were able to find the butter easily and eat it.

7. Īśitvam – The power to rule over all the three worlds. Śrī Hanumāna rules over everybody's hearts by his good deeds and character and not by physical might.

8. Vaśitvam – The power to control everybody, to make others follow you. Śrī Hanumāna's magnetic personality made everyone love him and obey him. This of course is true for the Lord. When He went to the forest, the entire city of Ayodhyā wanted to follow Him to the forest. When Śrī Kṛṣṇa played His flute, not only the Gopīs but even the cows and birds came to Him.

Even if we do not have supernatural powers we all need the below mentioned eight abilities to be successful and happy:

1. Aṇimā – The ability to become small or humble. Whilst crossing the ocean, Śrī Hanumāna came across the demoness, Surasā, who kept increasing her size to double his form. Śrī Hanumāna thought, 'If this goes on, the Lord's work will not get done. If I have to become small to accomplish my goal, so be it.' Assuming a small form he quickly enters and escapes from her widely opened mouth, even before she could close it. Śrī Rāma, even though was promised the princehood of Ayodhyā did not make a prestige issue when asked to go to the forest. He

happily renounced His royal attire and adorned simple clothes appropriate for an austere life in the forest.

2. Mahimā – The ability to become big or take on a leading or important role. When called upon, Śrī Hanumāna led the army of monkeys and performed the star role of finding Mother Sītā. Also, we should always think big and set high goals. If the goal itself is small, we achieve very little. Small scale jñāna-yajñas (series of spiritual discourses) were called mini–yajñas. The organizers thought small, did little and achieved almost nothing. The yajñas were renamed as area yajñas. Thereafter the whole area of a city was covered and its scope, scale and response became better.

3. Garimā – The ability to become heavy or firm in one's convictions or decisions. We should not get swayed easily or become confused or indecisive. By remaining firm in our knowledge, even the greatest of challenges or difficulties do not shake us.[1]

4. Laghimā – Be light–hearted and jovial. A bald man was given a comb as a parting gift. Instead of feeling insulted, he said, "Thank you! I shall never part with it!" Also we should learn to travel light. Some carry three huge suitcases for an overnight stay! We should not carry any emotional baggage or burden ourselves with worry or get bogged down by negative thinking, prejudices or opinions. Let us not assume to become the general manager of the world and learn to carry our responsibilities lightly. Svāmī Akhaṇḍānanda Mahārāja said about Pūjya Gurudev, "His knowledge is not a burden to him."

---

[1] *yasmin-sthito na duḥkhena guruṇāpi vicālyate – Gītā* VI.22

5. Prāpti – The ability to mobilize resources. A man needed Rs. 50 Lakhs to build his house. He had Rs. 25,000/– so he just built the bathroom! We must have the ability to procure the required wealth, material and know-how to complete a task. 'Everything is there in the world. One must work hard and get it'.[1] If 90% marks are required to get admission in a desired course, then one should work hard and get it.

6. Prākāmya – To be mobile and flexible. Some get stuck in a situation, position or place and are unable to come out of it or progress. The Upaniṣad says – keep moving (caraivaiti). The rigid tree, however huge, gets uprooted by the storm, whereas the flexible bamboo withstands all adversities. Also prākāmya is the ability to take on various roles as required by the situation and outshine in each of them. Śrī Rāma was an ideal son, husband, brother, ruler, student, friend and so on. Śrī Hanumāna took a back seat or the driver's role as per the situation.

7. Īśitvam – The ability to rule, manage, govern or execute a task. We should be able to reward or punish (anugraha–nigraha) as required and take the right decisions in a situation.

8. Vaśitvam – The ability to control others with love and understanding. The power of love is so great that even the Lord had to break His promise of not carrying weapons in the Mahābhārata war to fulfill the desire of His devotee, Bhīṣma.

---

[1] *sakala padārtha hai jaga māhiṁ, karma hina nara pāvata nāhiṁ*

By meditating on Śrī Hanumāna we also get the eight powers of intelligence, strength, good name, fortitude, fearlessness, good health, agility and eloquence.[1]

1. Buddhiḥ – Intelligence: That by which one can clearly and rightly understand what one should do and not do, what is right and wrong, what is one's duty and not one's duty, what to fear and not to fear and what binds and liberates.[2]

2. Balam – Strength: 'I am the strength amongst the strong devoid of desire and attachment'[3]. Such strength is His glory. True strength is the strength of character because of which one does not fall prey to temptations, compromise with values or waver from the path of righteousness. A great spiritual strength is required to realize the Truth. Without it one does not attain the supreme Self.[4]

3. Yaśaḥ – Good Name: When we die, only our name remains in the world. 'When we die, let our good name live on'[5]. Our name should become a source of inspiration to others, a 'brand' name which suggests greatness and which works wherever used. It is only by Pūjya Gurudev's name, the 'Chinmaya' brand that the Chinmaya Mission progresses. The Lord and His devotee's name are always great.

---

[1] *buddhir–balaṁ yaśo dhairyaṁ nirbhayatvaṁ arogatā,*
ajāḍyaṁ vāk–patutvaṁ ca hanumat smaraṇāt bhavet.

[2] *pravṛttiṁ ca nivṛttiṁ ca kāryākārye bhayābhaye,*
bandhaṁ mokṣaṁ ca yā vetti buddhiḥ sā pārtha sāttvikī. – (*Gītā* 18.30)

[3] *balaṁ balavatāṁ cāhaṁ kāma–raga–vivarjitam* – *Gītā* 7.11

[4] *nāyaṁ ātmā balahīnena labhyaḥ* – *Muṇḍakopaniṣad* 3.2.4

[5] *marāve pari kīrti rūpe urāve*

4. Dhairyam – Fortitude: Noble fortitude is the ability to unswervingly hold on to the right path till the goal is reached with full control over the mind and senses.[1] It is not to hold on to wrong notions or for selfish ends.

5. Nirbhayatvam – Fearlessness: It is a divine virtue (daivi sampatti). Walking on the path of righteousness makes us fearless (sāṅca ko āṅca nahiṁ). Immoral or criminal acts make us fearful. It is said that the mighty Rāvaṇa sneaked in like a frightened dog when he came to kidnap Mother Sītā. However, true fearlessness comes from total dispassion (vairāgyaṁ eva abhayaṁ) or when one realizes the non-dual Truth (advaita bhāva).

6. Arogatā – Good health: A healthy mind in a healthy body is truly our greatest wealth. People suffer due to physical and mental diseases. However, delusion about our true nature is the root of all afflictions. To realize the Self, good health (svasthatā) is essential as it eases out all diseases.

7. Ajāḍyam – Agility: Physical and mental laziness, spiritual stagnation and inertia in thinking are obstacles to progress. A mind that is vigilant, alert, bright, agile and flexible can achieve great goals.

8. Vāk paṭutvam – Eloquence: Unlike animals, man is blessed with speech. We should be careful and intelligent in what we speak. We should speak only where our words will be honoured.[2]

---

[1] *dhṛtyā yayā dhārayate manaḥ–prāṇendriyakriyāḥ,*
yogenāvyabhicāriṇyā dhṛtiḥ sā pārtha sāttvikī. – (*Gītā* 18.33)

[2] kiñca tattraiva vaktavyaṁ yatroktaṁ saphalaṁ bhavet

All quarrels arise due to words. Some never speak what they mean and never mean what they speak. Our words must be clear, without doubts, sweet, truthful and meaningful. Lord Rāma in His very first meeting with Śrī Hanumāna declared him to be an eloquent scholar (nava vyākaraṇa paṇḍita) as his words were clear, meaningful, with pleasing expressions and without unnecessary words.

The nine kinds of wealth and precious stones of Kubera are Mahāpadma, Padma, Śaṅkha, Makara, Kachapā, Mukunda, Kunda, Nīla and Kharva. However, the greatest wealth that Śrī Hanumāna gives us is the love for Lord Rāma (rāmarasa). Once you have that, you don't need any other wealth.

* * *

राम रसायन तुम्हरे पासा।
सदा रहो रघुपति के दासा ॥३२॥

rāma rasāyana tumhare pāsā,
sadā raho raghupati ke dāsā. (32)

32. The elixir of devotion to Lord Rāma is with you, who always stays with utmost humility at the feet of Lord Rāma as His servant.

तुम्हरे भजन राम को पावै।
जनम जनम के दुख बिसरावै ॥३३॥

tumhare bhajana rāma ko pāvai,
janama janama ke dukha bisarāvai. (33)

33. Singing your praise makes Lord Rāma bless that person and makes one forget the miseries of all previous births.

अंत काल रघुबर पुर जाई।
जहाँ जन्म हरि-भक्त कहाई ॥३४॥

anta kāla raghubara pura jāī,
jahām̐ janma hari-bhakta kahāī. (34)

34. At the end of one's life when one goes to the abode of Lord Rāma, such a person will be deemed as having been born as a devotee of Hari (Lord Rāma).

Mother Sītā said, "May you always serve Lord Rāma with great love and devotion – may you always be His dear servant. If anyone worships you, he automatically obtains Lord Rāma." Also Lord Rāma is happy if people praise Śrī Hanumāna. So this is the best way to please Lord Rāma. One who worships Śrī Hanumāna will have no sorrow. He will forget sorrows, not only of this life but all past lives also. Such a person at the time of death will go to the abode of Lord Rāma called Vaikuṇṭhaloka or Sāketaloka. Being devotees of Śrī Hanumāna they automatically become devotees of Lord Rāma. And what do these devotees do in the abode of the Lord? They just sit and watch the Lord and revel in His divine presence. Some say that it is unproductive to just watch the Lord and do nothing else. But these same people spend hours watching television! True devotees never grow tired of being in the presence of the Lord, who is the very embodiment of all beauty, kindness and compassion. In fact, devotees wish to be born again on this earth when the Lord incarnates, so that they can be with Him.

* * *

और देवता चित्त न धरई ।
हनुमत सेइ सर्ब सुख करई ॥३५॥

aura devatā citta na dharaī,
hanumata sei sarba sukha karaī . (35)

35. A devotee of Śrī Hanumāna need not worship any other deity, as by serving Śrī Hanumāna, he will surely get all happiness.

संकट कटै मिटै सब पीरा ।
जो सुमिरै हनुमत बलबीरा ॥३६॥

saṅkaṭa kaṭai miṭai saba pīrā,
jo sumirai hanumata balabīrā. (36)

36. All miseries and torments vanish when one remembers the brave Hanumāna.

Gosvāmī Tulasīdāsa says that we need not remember any other deities. Just remember Śrī Hanumāna and we will get all we need from him. What does this mean? One should have full faith in whoever one worships. We should have single pointed devotion. If we choose to worship Śrī Hanumāna with full faith, all our prayers will be answered. Another meaning of this verse is that some worship other deities like Lord Indra for worldly pleasures or success. But these deities are themselves full of desires. Lord Indra is always afraid that somone who does a lot of penance may take over the throne of his heavenly kingdom. Such deities may not answer our prayers. But Śrī Hanumāna's devotion for the Lord has no selfish desire. He is always engaged in serving others. So, he will always answer our prayers. Therefore we should worship him alone. All our problems, pains and sorrows will be eliminated.

* * *

जै जै जै हनुमान गोसाईं ।
कृपा करहु गुरु देव की नाईं ॥३७ ॥

jai jai jai hanumāna gosāīṁ,
kṛpā karahu guru deva kī nāīṁ. (37)

37. Victory to you! Victory to you! O Lord Hanumāna! Bless us with your grace as our preceptor.

Victory to Śrī Hanumāna who is a gosvāmī (gosāīṁ in Avadhi dialect). 'Gosvāmī 'in Sanskrit means one who has control over his senses. (go – sense organs + svāmī – master). Śrī Hanumāna can face any challenge and emerge victorious because he has full control over his body and mind. A person who is in full control of his/her senses and worships Śrī Hanumāna with devotion, will become victorious. No challenge is too big for such a person. Most of us have no control over our mind and we let it run here and there. Let us make it single pointed.

Nāīṁ means 'like' or 'similar to'. Śrī Hanumāna is like a Guru, a compassionate teacher. As we saw earlier, Śrī Hanumāna is an incarnation of Lord Śiva who is worshipped as the universal teacher (jagat Guru). Śrī Hanumāna is a compassionate Guru and one should learn from him. Another meaning of Guru is one who swallows the weaknesses of his students. Even if the student is foolish or commits mistakes, a true Guru will overlook it. He will help the students in overcoming their faults. So, worship of Śrī Hanumāna will help us overcome all our faults.

* * *

जो सत बार पाठ कर कोई।
छूटहि बंदि महा सुख होई ॥३८॥

jo sata bāra pāṭha kara koī,
chūṭahi bandi mahā sukha hoī. (38)

38. One who recites this *Hanumānacālīsā* a hundred times, is released from bondage – the cycle of birth and death – and enjoys absolute Bliss.

जो यह पढ़ै हनुमान चलीसा।
होय सिद्धि साखी गौरीसा ॥३९॥

jo yaha paḍhai hanumāna calīsā,
hoya siddhi sākhī gaurīsā. (39)

39. One who reads the *Hanumānacālīsā* regularly will accomplish his goals to which Lord Śiva is a witness.

One who reads this *Hanumānacālīsā* one hundred times will be released from all bondage and sorrows. Many recite the *Hanumānacālīsā* one hundred times on Tuesdays or Saturdays. It often takes six to seven hours. Some recite it continuously when they have problems or stress in their lives. Its chanting definitely gives relief from sorrow. One who reads *Hanumānacālīsā* attains perfection. Someone might say that it is a tall claim. How do we know that such a thing will happen? Gosvāmī Tulasīdāsa says that Lord Śiva (husband of Gaurī or Pārvatī) Himself is the witness. He will guarantee that you will attain perfection. How does one understand this? Chanting *Hanumānacālīsā* everyday will create noble thoughts in us. Then you will understand its real meaning which will help us purify our mind. Once we start our spiritual journey, all our energies get directed to this goal and with focussed efforts we will attain liberation. So we have to make a beginning somewhere. With diligence and effort, we will succeed.

* * *

तुलसीदास सदा हरि चेरा।
कीजै नाथ हृदय महँ डेरा ॥४०॥

tulasīdāsa sadā hari cerā,
kījai nātha hṛdaya mahaṁ ḍerā. (40)

40. O Hanumāna! I, Tulasīdāsa am always the servant of the Lord (Lord Rāma) and pray that you make your permanent residence in my heart.

Gosvāmī Tulasīdāsa who composed the *Hanumānacālīsā* considers himself to be a servant of Lord Hari, (Lord Rāma). Hari means one who removes all sufferings. He says, "Oh Lord! please stay in my heart and reside there always. Do not ever leave me."

* * *

दोहा

पवनतनय संकट हरन, मंगल मूरति रूप।
राम लखन सीता सहित, हृदय बसहु सुर भूप॥

dohā

pavanatanaya saṅkaṭa harana, maṅgala mūrati rūpa.
rāma lakhana sītā sahita, hṛdaya basahu sura bhūpa.

O! Son of Wind-god, destroyer of all miseries, you are an embodiment of auspiciousness. O King of gods! Do reside in my heart along with Lord Rāma, Lakṣmaṇa and Mother Sītā.

May Śrī Hanumāna dwell in my heart. The son of Wind-god who is the remover of all difficulties and whose very form is so auspicious, is the king of all gods. May he always dwell in my heart. Śrī Hanumāna will not be alone. Lord Rāma, Lakṣmaṇa and Mother Sītā are always with him! The Lord always resides wherever his devotee does. So, Lord Rāma will surely be in our heart along with Śrī Hanumāna. Also, as we saw earlier, Lord Rāma represents knowledge, Mother Sītā devotion, and Lakṣmaṇa dispassion. Śrī Hanumāna embodies all these qualities. Worship of Śrī Hanumāna will help inculcate these qualities in us also.

This is the glory (mahimā) of *Hanumānacālīsā*. Though it appears simple at first reading, recitation of it with understanding and devotion will result in great benefit. One should chant it at least once every day. That will help us purify our mind and guide us on the spiritual path and lead us to liberation.

Om Tat Sat

श्री हनुमान चालीसा

दोहा

श्रीगुरु चरन सरोज रज निज मनु मुकुरु सुधारि।
बरनउँ रघुबर बिमल जसु जो दायकु फल चारि ॥१॥
बुद्धिहीन तनु जानिके, सुमिरौं पवन-कुमार।
बल बुधि बिद्या देहु मोहिं, हरहु कलेस बिकार ॥२॥

चौपाई

जय हनुमान ज्ञान गुन सागर।
जय कपीस तिहुँ लोक उजागर ॥१॥
राम दूत अतुलित बल धामा।
अंजनि-पुत्र पवनसुत नामा ॥२॥
महाबीर बिक्रम बजरंगी।
कुमति निवार सुमति के संगी ॥३॥
कंचन बरन बिराज सुबेसा।
कानन कुंडल कुंचित केसा ॥४॥
हाथ बज्र औ ध्वजा बिराजै।
काँधे मूँज जनेऊ साजै ॥५॥
संकर सुवन केसरीनंदन।
तेज प्रताप महा जग बंदन ॥६॥
बिद्यावान गुनी अति चातुर।
राम काज करिबे को आतुर ॥७॥

प्रभु चरित्र सुनिबे को रसिया ।
राम लषन सीता मन बसिया ॥८ ॥
सूक्ष्म रूप धरि सियहिं दिखावा ।
बिकट रूप धरि लंक जरावा ॥९ ॥
भीम रूप धरि असुर सँहारे ।
रामचन्द्र के काज सँवारे ॥१० ॥
लाय सजीवन लखन जियाये ।
श्रीरघुबीर हरषि उर लाये ॥११ ॥
रघुपति कीन्ही बहुत बड़ाई ।
तुम मम प्रिय भरतहि सम भाई ॥१२ ॥
सहस बदन तुम्हरो जस गावैं ।
अस कहि श्रीपति कण्ठ लगावैं ॥१३ ॥
सनकादिक ब्रह्मादि मुनीसा ।
नारद सारद सहित अहीसा ॥१४ ॥
जम कुबेर दिगपाल जहाँ ते ।
कबि कोबिद कहि सके कहाँ ते ॥१५ ॥
तुम उपकार सुग्रीवहिं कीन्हा ।
राम मिलाय राज पद दीन्हा ॥१६ ॥
तुम्हरो मन्त्र बिभीषन माना ।
लंकेस्वर भए सब जग जाना ॥१७ ॥
जुग सहस्र जोजन पर भानु ।
लील्यो ताहि मधुर फल जानू ॥१८ ॥
प्रभु मुद्रिका मेलि मुख माहीं ।
जलधि लाँघि गये अचरज नाहीं ॥१९ ॥
दुर्गम काज जगत के जेते ।
सुगम अनुग्रह तुम्हरे तेते ॥२० ॥
राम दुआरे तुम रखवारे ।
होत न आज्ञा बिनु पैसारे ॥२१ ॥

सब सुख लहै तुम्हारी सरना।
तुम रच्छक काहू को डर ना ॥२२॥
आपन तेज सम्हारो आपै।
तीनों लोक हाँक तें काँपै ॥२३॥
भूत पिसाच निकट नहिं आवै।
महाबीर जब नाम सुनावै ॥२४॥
नासै रोग हरै सब पीरा।
जपत निरंतर हनुमत बीरा ॥२५॥
संकट तें हनुमान छुड़ावै।
मन क्रम बचन ध्यान जो लावै ॥२६॥
सब पर राम तपस्वी राजा।
तिन के काज सकल तुम साजा ॥२७॥
और मनोरथ जो कोइ लावै।
सोइ अमित जीवन फल पावै ॥२८॥
चारों जुग परताप तुम्हारा।
है परसिद्ध जगत उजियारा ॥२९॥
साधु संत के तुम रखवारे।
असुर निकंदन राम दुलारे ॥३०॥
अष्ट सिद्धि नौ निधि के दाता।
अस बर दीन जानकी माता ॥३१॥
राम रसायन तुम्हरे पासा।
सदा रहो रघुपति के दासा ॥३२॥
तुम्हरे भजन राम को पावै।
जनम जनम के दुख बिसरावै ॥३३॥
अंत काल रघुबर पुर जाई।
जहाँ जन्म हरि-भक्त कहाई ॥३४॥
और देवता चित्त न धरई।
हनुमत सेइ सर्ब सुख करई ॥३५॥

संकट कटै मिटै सब पीरा ।
जो सुमिरै हनुमत बलबीरा ॥३६ ॥
जै जै जै हनुमान गोसाईं ।
कृपा करहु गुरु देव की नाईं ॥३७ ॥
जो सत बार पाठ कर कोई ।
छूटहि बंदि महा सुख होई ॥३८ ॥
जो यह पढ़ै हनुमान चलीसा ।
होय सिद्धि साखी गौरीसा ॥३९ ॥
तुलसीदास सदा हरि चेरा ।
कीजै नाथ हृदय महँ डेरा ॥४० ॥

दोहा

पवनतनय संकट हरन, मंगल मूरति रूप ।
राम लखन सीता सहित, हृदय बसहु सुर भूप ॥
सियावर रामचन्द्र की जय
पवनसुत हनुमान की जय
उमापति महादेव की जय
बोलो भई सब संतन की जय

Śrī Hanumāna Cālīsā

dohā

śrīguru carana saroja raja nija manu mukuru sudhāri,
baranauṁ raghubara bimala jasu jo dāyaku phala cāri. (1)
buddhihīna tanu jānike, sumirau pavana-kumāra,
bala budhi bidyā dehu mohiṁ, harahu kalesa bikāra. (2)

caupāī

jaya hanumāna jñāna guna sāgara,
jaya kapīsa tihuṁ loka ujāgara. (1)
rāma dūta atulita bala dhāmā,
añjani-putra pavanasuta nāmā. (2)
mahābīra bikrama bajaraṅgī,
kumati nivāra sumati ke saṅgī. (3)
kañcana barana birāja subesā,
kānana kuṇḍala kuñcita kesā. (4)
hātha bajra au dhvajā birājai,
kāṁdhe mūṁja janeū sājai. (5)
saṅkara suvana kesarīnandana,
teja pratāpa mahā jaga bandana. (6)
bidyāvāna gunī ati cātura,
rāma kāja karibe ko ātura. (7)

prabhu caritra sunibe ko rasiyā,
rāma laṣana sītā mana basiyā. (8)
sūkṣma rūpa dhari siyahiṁ dikhāvā,
bikaṭa rūpa dhari laṅka jarāvā. (9)
bhīma rūpa dhari asura saṁ̐hāre,
rāmacandra ke kāja saṁ̐vāre. (10)
lāya sajīvana lakhana jiyāye,
śrīraghubīra haraṣi ura lāye. (11)
raghupati kīnhī bahuta baḍāī,
tuma mama priya bharatahi sama bhāī. (12)
sahasa badana tumharo jasa gāvaiṁ,
asa kahi śrīpati kaṇṭha lagāvaiṁ. (13)
sanakādika brahmādi munīsā,
nārada sārada sahita ahīsā. (14)
jama kubera digapāla jahāṁ̐ te,
kabi kobida kahi sake kahāṁ̐ te. (15)
tuma upakāra sugrīvahiṁ kīnhā,
rāma milāya rāja pada dīnhā. (16)
tumharo mantra bibhīṣana mānā,
laṅkesvara bhae saba jaga jānā. (17)
juga sahasra jojana para bhānu,
līlyo tāhi madhura phala jānū. (18)
prabhu mudrikā meli mukha māhīṁ,
jaladhi lāṁ̐ghi gaye acaraja nāhīṁ. (19)
durgama kāja jagata ke jete,
sugama anugraha tumhare tete. (20)
rāma duāṛe tuma rakhavāre,
hota na ājñā binu paisāre. (21)

saba sukha lahai tumhārī saranā
tuma racchaka kāhū ko ḍara nā . (22)
āpana teja samhāro āpai,
tīnoṁ loka hāṁka teṁ kāṁpai. (23)
bhūta pisāca nikaṭa nahim āvai,
mahābīra jaba nāma sunāvai. (24)
nāsai roga harai saba pīrā,
japata nirantara hanumata bīrā. (25)
saṅkaṭa teṁ hanumāna chuḍāvai,
mana krama bacana dhyāna jo lāvai. (26)
saba para rāma tapasvī rājā,
tina ke kāja sakala tuma sājā. (27)
aura manoratha jo koi lāvai,
soi amita jīvana phala pāvai. (28)
cāroṁ juga paratāpa tumhārā,
hai parasiddha jagata ujiyārā. (29)
sādhu santa ke tuma rakhavāre,
asura nikandana rāma dulāre. (30)
aṣṭa siddhi nau nidhi ke dātā,
asa bara dīna jānakī mātā. (31)
rāma rasāyana tumhare pāsā,
sadā raho raghupati ke dāsā. (32)
tumhare bhajana rāma ko pāvai,
janama janama ke dukha bisarāvai. (33)
anta kāla raghubara pura jāī,
jahāṁ janma hari-bhakta kahāī. (34)
aura devatā citta na dharaī,
hanumata sei sarba sukha karaī . (35)

saṅkaṭa kaṭai miṭai saba pīrā,
jo sumirai hanumata balabīrā. (36)
jai jai jai hanumāna gosāīṁ,
kṛpā karahu guru deva kī nāīṁ. (37)
jo sata bāra pāṭha kara koī,
chūṭahi bandi mahā sukha hoī. (38)
jo yaha paḍhai hanumāna calīsā,
hoya siddhi sākhī gaurīsā. (39)
tulasīdāsa sadā hari cerā,
kījai nātha hṛdaya mahaṁ ḍerā. (40)

dohā

pavanatanaya saṅkaṭa harana, maṅgala mūrati rūpa.
rāma lakhana sītā sahita, hṛdaya basahu sura bhūpa.
siyāvara rāmacandra kī jaya
pavanasuta hanumāna kī jaya
umāpati mahādeva kī jaya
bolo bhaī saba santana kī jaya

हनुमान-स्तुति

हौं तुम्हारो एक दास गोसाई कृपा करो हनुमान ॥धृ ॥

सिद्धबाड़ी की तपोभूमि में आप बिराजे वीरासनमें
सब में जगाते भाव भक्ति के अगणित गुण के निधान ॥१ ॥

राम प्राण सेवा ही जीवन दुष्ट विमर्दन साधु संरक्षण
सब में करे शक्ति का प्रगटन अतुलित बल के निधान ॥२ ॥

आराधन नित वंदन कीर्तन और करुँ मैं नम्र निवेदन
जीवन हो हम सबका पावन दिव्य हो आप समान ॥३ ॥

स्वामी तेजोमयानंद

Hanumāna-Stuti

haum̐ tumhāro eka dāsa gosāī kṛpā karo hanumāna (dhṛ)

siddhabāḍī kī tapobhūmi meṁ āpa birāje vīrāsanameṁ
saba meṁ jagāte bhāva bhakti ke agaṇita guṇa ke nidhāna (1)

rāma prāṇa sevā hī jīvana duṣṭa vimardana sādhu saṁrakṣaṇa
saba meṁ kare śakti kā pragaṭana atulita bala ke nidhāna (2)

ārādhana nita vandana kīrtana aura karum̐ maiṁ namra nivedana
jīvana ho hama sabakā pāvana divya ho āpa samāna (3)

Swami Tejomayananda